Scarborough's War Years
IN OLD PHOTOGRAPHS

Clarence Gardens. With the construction of the North Promenade in the 1880s work was also put in hand to develop the undercliff. The Clarence Gardens were laid out in honour of Prince Albert, Duke of Clarence who visited Scarborough to open the Royal Albert Drive in 1890.

Scarborough's War Years

IN OLD PHOTOGRAPHS

Collected by

RICHARD JAMES PERCY

Alan Sutton Publishing
Phoenix Mill · Far Thrupp
Stroud · Gloucestershire

First published 1992

Copyright © Richard James Percy, 1992

British Library Cataloguing
in Publication Data

Percy, Richard James
Scarborough's War Years in Old Photographs
I. Title
942.847084

ISBN 0-7509-0238-8

Typeset in 9/10 Sabon.
Typesetting and origination by
Alan Sutton Publishing Limited
Printed in Great Britain

Royal Field Artillery. Three soldiers of the local territorials, the 5th Yorkshire Regiment are seen here at St Johns Road Barracks before being sent to the front. From the left are Thomas Pottage and Freddy Ireland, both later killed in France.

Contents

Introduction

The early years of the twentieth century saw Scarborough confident in her position as a premier seaside resort. The hotels and boarding houses were crowded with the middle-class holiday-maker who had largely replaced the landed gentry who, since the seventeenth century, had come to take the waters.

The entertainment was plentiful. Will Catlin's Pierrots were on the South Sands, the Fol-de-Rols were playing to full houses at the newly opened Floral Hall and, for those desiring a more cultural programme, the Grand Opera House, Theatre Royal and the Londesborough Theatre were staging plays and light opera.

On 4 August 1914 Great Britain declared war upon Germany, but, at a first glance, one would have been forgiven for thinking that the country was still at peace. The visitors remained and there was no panic-stricken departure. The only sign of the critical situation was the long queues of young men at the Army recruitment offices. The atmosphere in Scarborough was relaxed; the residents and visitors felt safe knowing that the Royal Navy, the most powerful in the world, was guarding the shores. This understandable illusion was shattered on Wednesday 16 December 1914; a day that was to send shock waves through the British Isles.

At 8.00 a.m. two German battle-cruisers, the *Derrflinger* and the *Von Der Tann* accompanied by the light cruiser, *Kolberg*, slowly and silently steamed out of the early morning mist and closed to within 1 mile of the resort. The *Kolberg* turned and made off in a southerly direction laying mines as she went. The two powerful battle-cruisers trained their 11 and 12 in guns upon the castle where they knew the signal station was situated. Their first salvoes reduced this building to a heap of rubble. The Germans were wary as they were under the impression that Scarborough was a fortified town. In actual fact the town had no defence whatsoever, unless the enemy regarded four eighteenth-century cannon that stood in the castle yard as a threat. Seeing that their fire was not returned the warships moved in nearer to the shore. Their large guns and secondary armament swung round and with a terrific roar opened up a steady fire on the peaceful town. After half an hour of concentrated fire the ships turned and steamed off as quickly and as silently as they had appeared.

Within that half hour 520 shells had exploded resulting in the deaths of 18 people including 8 women and 4 children. Over 210 buildings had been damaged or destroyed including 10 public buildings, 7 churches and 5 hotels. The town was in turmoil. People were running from house to house shouting that the Germans were coming. Panic set in and whole families hastily packed a few essential belongings and made their way out into the surrounding villages. Some just wandered about in a daze. One man on seeing a woman dressed in only a vest walking up the street shouted, 'Nay lass, come on, be decent.'

The 8th West Yorkshire Regiment who were billeted in York were quickly mobilized and arrived in Scarborough at 2.30 p.m. They positioned themselves at strategic points throughout the town but by that time the Germans were safely back in their home base after successfully evading Beatty's squadron that had steamed to intercept them.

Slowly the residents of Scarborough returned to their homes but a feeling of unease had crept into their everyday life. Would it happen again was the big question. As the months passed by people grew a little more confident and even when Zeppelins appeared overhead there was little worry, due perhaps to the fact that everyday folk did not appreciate the dangers of these airships. The Zeppelins were obviously after bigger targets because the nearest bomb that was dropped to Scarborough landed harmlessly at Seamer. Then on 6 September 1917 the people's deep-rooted fears materialized.

At 6.45 p.m. an enemy U-Boat appeared 4 miles off Scarborough. It lay there for about 15 minutes before opening fire. Of the thirty rounds fired, half of the shells fell among fishing and pleasure boats in the bay causing little or no damage. The other half exploded on land resulting in the deaths of three people and injuring another five. A number of minesweepers which were anchored in the bay raised steam and set off in pursuit but by the time they reached the submarine's position it had submerged.

The following year on 11 November 1918 the Prime Minister announced that the Armistice had been signed and that from 11 a.m. all hostilities were to cease. Thanksgiving services were held throughout the town and prayers said for the families of the 636 local men who up to that date were known to have been killed. The following year on 19 July 1919 Peace Sunday was celebrated with firework displays from the pier and from the boats in the bay. There was dancing on the Spa to Alick Maclean's Orchestra and at 11 p.m. the celebrations were rounded off by the lighting of the ancient beacon on the castle wall. It had been the war to end war, the boys were returning home and the future looked secure.

The years leading up to the Second World War witnessed large scale development taking place in an effort to create a resort second to none. The North Side, until then a quiet and rural backwater, was made popular with the holidaymaker by the laying out of parks and gardens. By 1931 and '32 the Miniature Railway and Open Air Theatre were operating and the opening of the North Bay Swimming Pool in 1938 marked the final stage of the project. In the old town whole streets of quaint cottages were demolished, and although a certain amount of rebuilding did take place, for the most part the open spaces were either grassed over or turned into car parks. On the outskirts of the town large estates sprang up and where once only green fields connected Scarborough to the outlying villages of Throxemby, Newby and Scalby the building programme had created a new suburbia. By the end of the decade Scarborough was being hailed as the 'Queen of the Yorkshire Coast'.

During August 1939 the situation in Europe had become critical and the threat of war was very real. On 1 September the first batch of evacuees began to arrive in Scarborough from Hull, Middlesborough and West Hartlepool. Over the following days over 14,000 refugee families would be billeted throughout the town.

Hostilities with Germany commenced on 3 September 1939 and Scarborough became a prohibited area. The sands, promenades and cliffs became restricted zones with deadly anti-personnel mines laid. All the main roads leading into town were barricaded off and patrolled by armed soldiers. It was a foolish person indeed who ventured into these places. Two young people did lose their lives by ignoring the warning signs and trespassing onto dangerous ground.

Scarborough's tourist trade suffered, not from the closure of its places of entertainment – they were to reopen in a day or two – but from the lack of accommodation. Every hotel and boarding-house was requisitioned by the military and occupied by the armed forces who remained there for the duration.

From the commencement of hostilities there was much enemy air activity along the coast and Scarborough's trawlers were often the target for marauding bombers. The resort's first air-raid warning wailed out at 9.25 a.m. on 29 January 1940 when German aircraft were spotted flying over Cayton Bay. On this occasion no incident occurred but over the following months the town was subjected to tip and run raids which although causing little damage did result in loss of life. The heaviest raid that Scarborough had to endure occurred on 18 March 1941. The raid, which became known as the 'March Blitz', began at 8.10 p.m. when ninety-eight aircraft flew in over the district and showered the Wold villages of Flixton and Folkton with incendiaries. They then closed in upon Scarborough at 9.00 p.m. and subjected the town to 2 hours of heavy indiscriminate bombing with high explosives, parachute mines and thousands of incendiaries. There then followed sporadic attacks when parachute mines were dropped. The 'All Clear' finally sounded at 4.37 a.m. the following day. It had been a trying night and the wartime services had been stretched to their limit. At one point the situation became so critical that the AFS had to call for assistance and appliances were rushed in from other districts to deal with the many fires.

After this devastating raid it was found that 1,378 buildings had either been damaged or destroyed. The loss of life was high with 27 fatalities including 4 babies, 5 children and 9 women, with a further 45 suffering varying degrees of injury.

Victory in Europe Day, 8 May 1945, brought the fear of air attack to an end. There had been twenty-one air raids on Scarborough with a further five machine-gun and cannon attacks. The casualties both military and civilian totalled 47 killed by bombs and mines and further 137 who suffered injury. Over 3,000 of the town's buildings had sustained damage from the bombing.

The following months saw the departure of the armed forces and de-requisitioning of the property taken over by the military. Even so, it was well into 1947 before the process was completed and even then the hotels and boarding-houses found difficulty in opening owing to the lack of soap and linen.

Post-war planning concentrated on the rehousing of families who had lost their homes during the course of the war. There were 2,460 applications for houses; 804 of the applicants had no home at all. The purchase of the Sandybed Estate had taken place in January 1945 and on 16 July twenty German prisoners of war started work on the erection of prefabricated buildings at Sandybed.

With the housing situation stablized, the next priority was the building up of the holiday trade. The wartime obstacles were cleared, the shows opened with the top names in the world of entertainment, and by the end of the 1940s Scarborough resumed her position as one of Britain's top seaside resorts.

SECTION ONE
Pre-1914

The rustic suburbs. These two cottages were so typical of Falsgrave at the turn of the century. On the far left of the photograph can be seen the old infants school that was opened in 1873.

A sedate mode of transport. The first cab to be seen on the streets of Scarborough appeared in 1836. By the early 1900s over two hundred cabs, landaus and hansoms were plying their trade. A feature of the season was the jockey carriage with the drivers dressed in silk blouses and racing colours. This photograph taken in Lower Prospect Road shows Tot Pottage in topper on the far left whose father was a cab proprietor.

The North Cliff. As the tourist trade began to increase in the mid-nineteenth century it became necessary to build lodging-houses for the middle-class visitors who were replacing the gentry who frequented the town less and less as the fashion for taking the waters declined. The Clarence Gardens Hotel seen on the far right and now renamed the Clifton Hotel, was the limit of development at the time of this photograph in about 1900. Beyond that were fields and allotments.

A premier show. The Fol-de-Rols were ranked for many years as one of the best shows in the country. They owed their existence to George Royle who in 1911 formed the troupe and booked them into the newly constructed Floral Hall. Many of the performers of later years – Arthur Askey, Reg Dixon, Ann Zeigler, Webster Booth and Jack Warner – have become household names.

The Grand Hotel. This imposing hotel with its prime position on St Nicholas Cliff allowing the guests unparalleled views along the coast was built between 1862 and 1867 to a design by Cuthbert Broderick. It has been described as being the most splendid of the 'Second Empire' hotels ever to be built in England. During the Second World War the RAF Initial Training Wing was billeted there.

The North Bay Pier. Built to a design by Mr Eugene Birch at a cost of £6,000, the 1,000 ft long promenade pier was opened in 1869. It proved to be popular with neither visitor nor local and the company soon ran into difficulties. It was bought by Mr W. Hudson of London who spent £10,000 on reconstruction work. He even erected a pavilion on the seaward end to try and lure the holiday-maker onto it. Mr Quentin Gibson, a well-known local entertainer, staged shows and refreshments were available. On the night of 7 January 1905 a terrible storm raged over the town. The next morning residents stared in disbelief at the pavilion standing marooned in the North Bay; the pier had completely vanished, washed away by the pounding seas.

A tranquil harbour scene. This view taken from the old pier at the turn of the century shows the magnificent sweep of the South Bay and outlines the imposing Grand Hotel in the distance. One of the oldest records of a pier at Scarborough dates back to the reign of Henry III when it was written that he granted a patent 'for making a new pier at Scardeburgh with timber and stone towards the sea'.

Sand-castles and rock pools. This quiet and secluded spot on the South Sands nestling beneath the South Cliff Gardens became known as 'Children's Corner'. The manager of the Prince of Wales Hotel was the prime mover in having the lift constructed in 1875. It worked on the principle of two tanks filling and emptying with water which resulted in the trams moving up and down. I doubt if the customer worried what system was in use as long as it saved them from having to climb the 224 steps to the Esplanade.

The Scarborough Pageant. This spectacular event staged in the castle yard in July 1912 was not a financial success although it proved to be very popular with the public. The reason for this was over-spending on a too-elaborate set-up. The person responsible for the show was F.G. Stapleton, vicar of Seamer, who persuaded a large group of local people to help him. It took sixteen months to prepare and No. 1 The Crescent was taken over for the making of the 1,000 costumes. Over 1,300 performers, both children and adults, played out various dramatic episodes. It was repeated again in August, this time with the added attraction of a grand procession through the streets.

Posing on the Spa in 1906. One can see that the bowler, watch-chain and high starched collar were definitely *de rigueur*. From left to right: John Pottage, a cab proprietor who at over fifty years of age became a sergeant in the Veterinary Corps during the First World War, Jack Howarth, a former booking clerk on the railways who, upon marrying a Sally Duck from the Pigeon Pie at Sherburn, took over a pub at Rillington and Frank Rielly, who was a staunch Catholic and served throughout the First World War in the East Yorkshire Regiment.

Credit allowed. Charles and Sarah Stokes are seen outside their shop at 1 Elders Street which they opened in 1902. No doubt they, as was the policy with most shops, offered credit with the customer paying at the end of the week. Notice the many brand names so familiar to this day.

Bathing machines. As far back as 1787 bathing machines could be seen on the South Sands. Two women attended each lady who bathed, and one man every gentleman. It was said that bathing on the sands caused great excitement and pleasure to the promenaders.

Spread Eagle Lane. This old property on the seaward side of Sandside consisting of warehouses, mast yards and run-down tenements was demolished in 1903/4 to create a wider thoroughfare with open views across the harbour. In the background can be seen the Lancaster Inn, still there to this day but greatly altered.

Open-air entertainment. Will Catlin's Pierrots first entertained on the South Sands in 1896. The corporation charged Will Catlin 6s per man per week for the stand. In 1909 Catlin built the Arcadia and here the troupe played to thousands of visitors each summer until the First World War.

Access to the Spa. In 1827 the Cliff Bridge was opened with great dash. Crowds cheered, a coach and horses sped at full speed over the bridge much to the consternation of genteel ladies who fainted with the excitement, and sumptuous dinners were laid on for the workmen. A toll was introduced at a later date and abolished in 1952 along with the toll-booths.

Victorian elegance. The Spa was, and still remains, the centre for first-class entertainment. During the First World War a German submarine captain often brought his craft in as near as possible to the Spa wall to listen to the night-time concerts given by Alick Maclean and his orchestra. After the war he wrote and said how much he had enjoyed his evenings on the Spa.

Holiday-makers' paradise. The popular Foreshore with its expanse of clean sand, pebble stalls and ice-cream vendors with their well-known cry of, 'Hokey Pokey, penny a lump, that's the stuff to make you jump' is depicted in this photograph taken at the turn of the century. Notice the ladies with their parasols to keep out the sun. A pure white complexion was the fashion and any hint of redness was regarded as being terribly common.

Victorian respectability. West Street on the exclusive South Cliff is pictured here in about 1900. It typifies an era before bed-sits and boarding-houses were the norm. The large villas were the homes of the gentry. Feniscowle House seen far left was the residence of Sir William Fieldon, Bart., with the house opposite being a private school for young ladies.

An early morning gossip. These two ladies standing outside their homes in Castlegate look a little vexed at having their privacy intruded upon. The property dates back to the 1790s but notice how spic and span everything looks. Every morning the carpets would be shaken and the steps scrubbed and whitestoned. Most of these houses were destroyed on 10 October 1940 when a land-mine exploded nearby.

Steady on the oars boys. Scarborough's Amateur Rowing Club was founded in 1869 and is now the oldest surviving club on the north-east coast. Originally the boats were made locally and were raced against coastguard boats in regattas. This photograph, taken in 1913, shows the members outside their headquarters on Foreshore Road prior to going on a picnic to Cayton Bay.

Naval visits. The Channel Squadron had a long association with Scarborough and their visits were greeted with much festivity. This photograph, taken in July 1906, shows a march past of sailors and the enthusiastic response of the spectators. In the background can be seen the battleships anchored in the bay. Over the years such famous battleships as *Barham*, *Hood*, *Malaya*, *Nelson* and *Royal Oak* have received a typical Scarborough welcome.

The idyllic charm of Scalby Mills drew both visitor and local alike to this favourite spot on the North Side. During the 1960s improvements took place and for a cost of £133,000 the promenade was extended, amusement arcades and a paddling pool built and a large car park constructed for the heavy traffic. The past few years have seen much controversy raging over the new sewerage plant that has been built there.

Cabmen disapprove. The first tram to run on Scarborough's streets did so on 6 May 1904. This caused great annoyance with the owners of horse-drawn conveyances who felt that their livelihood was being threatened. The trams proved not to be a financial success, however, and in March 1931 the corporation purchased the company for £19,000. The last tramcar ran from the West Pier to its depot on Scalby Road on Wednesday 30 September 1931.

Potted palms and floral displays were typical of the Floral Hall which was built in the Alexandra Gardens in 1910. In 1911 George Royle's famous Fol-de-Rols began their long association with the theatre. Over the years many big names have trodden the boards but even these premier shows did not sway the decision to close the building. It was demolished in the late 1980s and a bowling centre built on the site.

Picture hats and sailor suits were all the fashion for children before the First World War. Edith and Ernest Gibson pose for a studio photograph in 1913.

A family business. Corner shops, greatly missed by many today, were an everyday sight until the 1960s when the large supermarkets forced them out of business. In them one could buy anything from a corset to a bar of chocolate.

Take your partners. Whether it was the grand ball in the evening or the less formal tea dance the Spa was considered the place to be. As one can see by this photograph taken in 1912 in the glass-covered walkway above the Grand Hall, the One Step is all the rage. It is a puzzle just where the dancers found room to manoeuvre.

From taxis to coal. The Scarborough family business of J. Robinson & Sons, realizing that the future lay with the motorized mode of transport, took the lead by introducing the first taxi-cab service to the town in about 1910. They followed this up by introducing motor rullies which delivered their 'Economic Coals' as can be seen by this photograph taken near the Aquarium top in 1913.

Christmas fare. This magnificent display of poultry at Dent & Sons, fish and game dealers, 93 Westborough, in 1913 would be highly criticized today by the health authorities as being unhygienic. Even so, one cannot but admire the work and imagination that has gone into it.

Home on leave is Thomas Pottage of the 5th Yorkshire Regiment, RFA posing with his sisters, Minnie, Clara and Frances and brothers, Jack, George and Frederick in 1914. He was fatally gassed in France during the last year of the war.

The Clock Cafe in the South Cliff Gardens is as popular today as it was when it first opened in 1912/13. Posing for the camera in 1913 are the cafe staff. The only member of the staff known is sixteen-year-old Minnie Pottage kneeling first right who was a scholar at the Municipal School and who was working during her summer holidays.

St Nicholas House and Gardens were purchased by the corporation from the Woodall family in 1898 for £33,000. Work went ahead to convert the house into the town hall which was officially opened by the Princess Henry of Battenburg on 28 July 1903. The gardens were opened to the public and became an easy and picturesque means of access to the Foreshore from the town.

St Marys School. These happy schoolchildren photographed in 1912 with their teacher are possibly celebrating May Day. The only pupil known is Alice Stokes second from the left on the back row. The school which stood at the top of Queen Street was demolished in about 1970 and a car park now stands on the site.

The First World War

Defend the town. With the declaration of war upon Germany on 4 August 1914 all the main roads leading from the beach were barricaded off. Here we can see an example of the defences erected across Eastborough.

Wounded foreigners. As the bombardment grew in intensity patients at the Old Hospital, Friarsway, were quickly carried downstairs by the nurses as shrapnel ripped through the building. Nancy Louth, who was fifteen years old at the time, remembers looking out of the X-ray room window and seeing the sky looking 'like a ball of fire'. Wounded Belgian soldiers are seen here after the raid at the Royal Sea Bathing Infirmary, Foreshore Road.

For King and Country. Lines of recruits are seen here in 1914 in the station forecourt, all eager to do their bit. Some of the men certainly appear to be well past fighting age. In the background can be seen the Westlands Hotel which was demolished in about 1930.

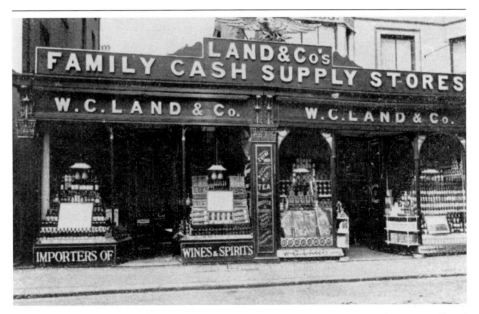

Loss of an employee. The high-class business of W.C. Land & Co., South Street suffered the loss of one of their assistants only minutes after the bombardment commenced. Mr Harry Frith was at the shop door as two shells burst further along the street killing him instantly. The business is long gone and forgotten by many but a descendant of the Land family only recently made headlines by being divorced by the Princess Royal.

A narrow escape. PC Hunter displays his shrapnel-riddled cape after a near miss by a shell. He had been on duty at the signal station on the Castle Hill when it came under fire from the German warships. Leaving his cape on the railings he had dived into the vaults of the Lady's Well for shelter along with the coastguards.

The first target of the German ships was the signal station in the castle grounds. Seen here after the bombardment with the ruins of the barracks in the background are those who were on duty at the time. Back row, left to right: A. Dean (chief officer), James Walsh, (boatman), L. Reeve (chief petty officer), Robert Barnes (leading boatman), PC H. Hunter, James Eastwood (trooper, Yorks. Yeomanry). Front row: Wilfred Durant (RNVR), George Mason (leading boatman), Harry Holden (RNVR).

Utter devastation. Broken plate-glass windows and valuable stock destroyed was the result of a shell bursting outside the premises of Charles Smith, Antique Dealer, Nos 1 and 3 South Street. Across the road at Clare & Hunt's Chemist an employee was killed at the door. After the raid shutters were quickly put in place and one can read the slogan, 'are we downhearted, NO', that someone has chalked up.

Barracks destroyed. The last time these barracks in the castle grounds were occupied by regular troops was in 1878. At the time of the bombardment they were being used as a store.

The last shot of the bombardment was fired shortly after 8.30 a.m. and hit the lighthouse tower. The damage to the building was so severe that the tower had to be taken down. Scarborough remained without a lighthouse tower until 1931 when the Scarborough Townsmen's Association had raised enough funds to rebuild it.

Tragedy strikes. One of the last shots fired by the German ships hit No. 2 Wykeham Street where seven people were living. It caused utter devastation and resulted in the deaths of Mrs Johanna Bennett, her son Albert, George Barnes and John Christopher Ward.

Belvedere, the home of George Lord Beeforth on the Esplanade, shows the scars caused by bursting shells. In time this house was taken over by Sir Eric Ohlson. Today the house has been tastefully converted into flats.

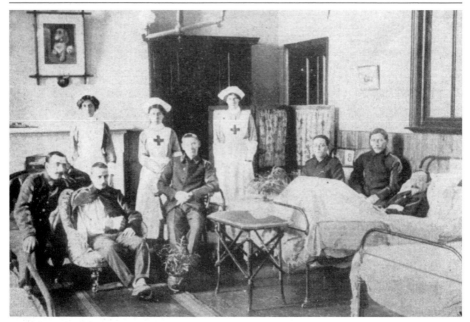

Hospital shelled. As wounded soldiers recovered from their injuries at the Royal Sea Bathing Infirmary on the Foreshore their rest was interrupted by the sound of exploding shells as the bombardment commenced. Nurses quickly carried them to safety from the top floor only seconds before a shell burst where they had been. Here we see them after their ordeal looking cheerful after narrowly escaping death.

Fatalities on Filey Road. Dunollie, Filey Road, the stately residence of John Henry Turner, a former Sheriff of Yorkshire, received no fewer than seventeen hits by shells. The servants and master took shelter in the boiler house but the maid, thirty-year-old Margaret Briggs was still working in the library. On hearing the postman Alfred Beal about to deliver the post she set off to collect it. At that moment a shell burst on the porch sending shrapnel flying in all directions. Both Alfred and Margaret were killed instantly.

Glad to be away. No. 14 Lonsdale Road was one of the first houses hit in the shelling but luckily the residents were away at the time.

Grand no more. Shells quickly reduced the façade of the Grand Restaurant and Picture House on the Foreshore to a shambles as the first salvo raked the front. Everything inside was destroyed except, it was said, a decanter of wine.

The first salvoes of shells burst along the Foreshore causing damage to the façade of the Olympia Picture House.

Shopkeeper killed. Mrs Emily Merryweather, aged 80, of No. 43 Prospect Road opened the door of her shop to admit two frightened ladies who were caught out in the raid. Just as she did so a shell exploded with terrific force in front of her causing fatal injuries. The shop was demolished in the late 1980s and a new building erected.

Elegant Belvoir Terrace was designed by
Richard and Samuel Sharp of York in 1833. A
shell scored a direct hit on No. 6 Belvoir
Terrace seriously injuring a young woman.

Georgian houses wrecked. Property at the rear
of St Nicholas Parade shows the damage that
fire from 12 in guns can cause.

Discovered hours later. A shell completely wrecked the home of Mr Charles Herbert at 79 Commercial Street. A woman in her eighties and her daughter, Jane White, who was injured in the back, were discovered at 3 p.m. – some seven hours after the raid began. The house suffered the same fate in the Second World War when a bomb exploded alongside it.

Holiday camp hit. Soldiers of the Territorial Army stand guard outside the ruins of the Kingscliff Holiday Camp on King Street after the bombardment.

Hotels suffer damage. The South Cliff facing the sea was an easy target for the German gunners. The many hotels and boarding-houses in the area received the full force of the shelling. The Red Lea Hotel, pictured here, on Prince of Wales Terrace shows its scars after the bombardment. The Prince of Wales Hotel that stands nearby sustained over £4,000 worth of damage during the raid.

Member of Parliament's home hit. Scarborough MP Mr Walter Russell Rea had a narrow escape when his residence at No. 7 The Crescent received a direct hit. His next door neighbour, Mr Micklethwaite, was equally lucky when his room on the second floor was reduced to a shambles. It was due to Mr Rea that the owners of damaged property received compensation from the Government.

The homes of both the rich and poor suffered damage in the bombardment. The utter devastation caused by a blast can be seen in this photograph of the front room of a house on the Esplanade.

Seven churches in the town were struck by shells during the half-hour bombardment. At All Saints on Falsgrave a shell came through the roof causing the damage seen in the photograph.

The Royal Hotel on St Nicholas Street received an unlucky hit from a shell that struck the town hall opposite and ricocheted over the road.

The Grand Hotel's imposing silhouette was an easy target for the Germans. Over thirty-six shells smashed into the building causing £13,000 worth of damage.

Chemist's shop wrecked. Clare & Hunt's Chemist at the corner of South Street received a direct hit and an employee, Leonard Ellis, who was standing in the doorway was killed.

The royal suite at the Royal Hotel where the Duke of Clarence had stayed was completely wrecked by a shell, as were over 150 windows.

Long Greece Steps leading up from Sandside is typical of the many alleyways and steps that lead up from the beach to the town. After the bombardment soldiers stationed themsleves at these points to guard against any possible invasion.

Another view of Long Greece Steps taken from Quay Street shows the houses to be in fairly good condition. This did not prevent the demolition of this property in the 1960s.

The funeral procession of Mrs Bennett and her family, killed in Wykeham Street during the bombardment, winds its way along Dean Road to the cemetery accompanied by soldiers of the 5th Yorkshire Regiment.

Sandbags for the front. Local fisherfolk under the supervision of Miss Barker of Grosvernor Bank, are seen here outside the Seamen's Institute, Sandside, where they did their bit for the war effort by making sandbags. By the end of 1914 they had produced over 180 which had been forwarded to the depot at Leeds.

Sunday best. Three-year-old Frances Pottage, seen here in 1917, is clutching her favourite toy.

A sailor's life. This photograph taken in 1915 shows Jack Pottage in his sea scout's uniform. The sea scouts' school was established in that same year by the borough council at St Thomas's Schoolroom, Tuthill. On 8 July 1918 Christopher Colborne Graham gave his Paradise Estate to Scarborough. and in the following September the sea scouts transferred from their old premises to Paradise House which became known as the Graham Sea Training School. Jack Pottage went on to serve in the Merchant Navy, was torpedoed twice on Atlantic convoys during the Second World War, and survived to become a bosun.

Before and after. The Centenary Chapel on Queen Street was built in 1839 on the site of the Blacksmiths Arms pub at a cost of £7,000. On 15 February 1915 one of the biggest fires to occur in Scarborough broke out and destroyed the chapel, Boyes Remnant Warehouse and other property in the vicinity. It was to be about six years before enough money could be raised to build a new chapel.

Women volunteers. Little is known about this photograph. It is obviously a local volunteer force. The only person known is Mrs Martha Gibson who is second from the right on the back row.

Never too old. At over fifty years of age John Pottage enlisted as a non-combatant with the 93rd Battery, RFA 280 Brigade, 56th Division, as a sergeant in the Veterinary Corps and served throughout the war in France.

New battery. In 1915 an appeal went out to lord mayors and mayors to raise artillery and engineer units to serve with the Pals' Batteries which had been recruited in various other parts of the country for Kitchener's army. Here in Scarborough the mayor undertook the responsibility of raising the Scarborough Battery and recruiting commenced on 17 March 1915. The official name for the Scarborough unit was 'C' Battery, 161st (Yorkshire) Brigade, RFA although it was more generally known as 'The Scarborough Pals' Battery'. Here they pose in the yard of St Johns Road Barracks.

Scarborough Castle was used as a training
ground for the local regiments who could
often be seen scaling the walls.

Local lads of the Territorial Army, the 5th Yorkshire, RFA march into the railway station
in 1915 *en route* to Darlington where they were to undertake an intensive training course
before leaving for the front. Notice the now demolished Pavilion Hotel in the background.

Patriotic feelings ran high on this Sunday morning in 1915 as the bright uniforms of the local 'Terriers' – the 5th Yorks. – proudly marched along Castle Road in the church parade, which was held in conjunction with the Scarborough Company of the National Reserve.

For displaying conspicuous courage under heavy fire when repairing telephone wires and for ministering to the wounded, Signaller Albert Midgley of the Scarborough Pals' Battery was awarded the Military Medal.

Officers and men of the Scarborough Pals' Battery pose for the camera outside the castle keep in 1915. Back row, left to right: Sgt. G. Whittaker, Cpl. Hopkins, Bdr. H. Rymer, Bdr. C. Vietch, Cpl. H. Salter, Sgt. A. Dawson, Bdr. H. Noble. Front row: Cpl. J. Welburn, Sgt.-Maj. H. Blackburn, Second Lieut. R. Gorle, Lieut. T. Kay (commanding officer), QMS W. Bland, Cpl. J. Welburn.

Preliminary training. Local lads of the 5th Yorks. take a well-earned rest from the intensive training at a camp near Darlington. The only known face is Thomas Pottage standing first right.

The Terriers. Young Scarborough lads of the 5th Yorks. are seen marching along an unidentified street in the town prior to their being sent to the front. Many would not see Scarborough again.

An official photograph of the 5th Yorks. taken at St Johns Road Barracks in 1914.

To raise money towards a sum of £100,000 which was the cost of building a submarine, Scarborough's Submarine Week began on Monday 4 March 1918. The tram which had been skilfully camouflaged as a submarine by Councillor Malton, stood outside the Pavilion Hotel. By the end of the week £127,514 had been raised.

The war to end wars. Scarborough celebrated peace on Saturday 19 June 1919 with bunting and flags flying. Large crowds of spectators gathered to watch schoolchildren parade in fancy dress. Warships in the bay fired off rockets and at night an impressive firework display lighted up the sky.

The Inter-war Years

The Theatre Royal, St Thomas Street, the town's oldest theatre, was closed down in 1924 and demolished shortly afterwards. It had been built between the years 1733 and 1767 and during 1869 and 1871 was honoured by the presence of HRH The Prince of Wales. Today there is no sign of the building except for a plaque erected by the Heritage Trust which gives details of the theatre.

Sun-tanned skins were definitely not the fashion when Minnie Pottage reached the age of 21 in 1918. It was only countrywomen who spent their time working in the open air who had red faces. A touch of *Poudre d'Amour*, which came in three tints, *Blande*, *Naturelle* and *Rachel* at 1s a box, and was said to enliven the most faded of skins, was acceptable.

An afternoon stroll along Sandside in 1920 was a peaceful pastime in the days before amusement arcades, fish and chip shops and ice-cream parlours were the fashion. Pushing their prams are from left to right: Lily Kelly, Clara Cooper and Cissie Peason with their babies Rene, Robert and Colin.

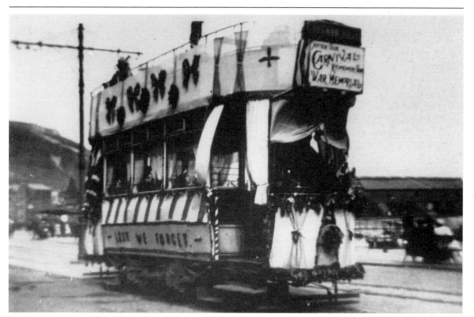

A tramcar travelling along the Foreshore advertises a carnival to raise money for the town's war memorial. The building of the memorial, which was eventually erected and unveiled on 26 September 1923, was financed entirely by voluntary subscription.

The American Bar at the Pavilion Hotel was a great favourite with both guest and local alike. The Pavilion Hotel which was built to a design by William Baldwin Stewart in 1870 was demolished in 1973. Perhaps one of its main claims to fame is that Charles Laughton's family were one-time owners and did much to popularize it.

The Lounge,
decoration by
B. S. Turner.

Another view of the Pavilion Hotel shows the lounge decorated in typical 1930s style by Mr B.S. Turner. The lounge, it was said, had soft lighting, welcoming armchairs and an air of distinction without being flamboyant.

This toast-rack bus was certainly a novelty when this photograph was taken in the station forecourt. Note the solid rubber tyres.

The elegant Spa which was opened by the Mayor of London on Bank Holiday Monday 1880 has always been a favourite centre for those wishing for light music, afternoon teas or just to sit on the verandahs and balconies. This view taken in about 1923 captures the atmosphere of a more relaxed era.

Spreight Lane Steps in the old town was not a place to loiter according to the residents of the area. On dark winter's nights when the gas lights flickered mysterious figures could be seen promenading up and down the street. An old woman lived nearby who, it was said, 'Lived on the vital breath of sick children'.

Dumple Street was demolished in 1930 and when rebuilt took the name of Friargate. The original street was one of the most colourful in town and had many characters. Seen on the left is Chapman's grocers where one could buy a bladder of lard. The lady in the photograph is standing outside Alice Hartley's shop and further down was Lizzie Richardson's shop, famous for her hot cakes and bacon at 2d a portion.

Charabanc trips were a popular pastime in the 1920s and on this particular outing taken at the Aquarium top are the regulars of the Ship Inn, Falsgrave. The landlord of the pub, Harry Gill, is seen seated second right with Albert Midgley, a future landlord, seated next to him.

Peasholm Lake had been constructed before the First World War on an area of land known locally as Tucker's Field. The joys of a relaxing afternoon in a canoe on the lake were as popular in the 1920s as they are today.

A tramcar decorated to advertise the cricket festival is standing in Scalby Road depot waiting to take to the road.

Taken on Burniston Road in the early 1930s, this photograph of an outing in the popular 3-wheeler Morgan shows a lady at the wheel, which was not a common sight in those days.

An afternoon stroll in Northstead Manor Gardens in the early 1920s shows the tranquillity of the area. During the early 1930s the gardens were developed to attract the visitor. Behind the bushes on the photograph is the route which the miniature railway would take.

The Cliff Bridge leading to the Spa was opened in 1827. Today many people know it as the Spa Bridge but its purpose is the same, to allow easy access to the Spa and the Esplanade.

These three lady bathers on the South Sands in the early 1930s dressed in very becoming costumes appear to be the only ones on the beach. In the background can be seen the Cliff Bridge, Gala Land and the Esplanade Hotel.

The Pavilion Hotel dominates this photograph taken about 1922. There is no roundabout and no Northway. The gentleman standing in the middle of the road is Robert Birley who was the tram inspector and who also changed the points if the need arose.

Silver fox furs were the height of fashion when Mrs Minnie Midgley posed for this photograph in about 1926. Victorian ladies had fainted with shock when hemlines rose to show the ankle in Edwardian times. Goodness knows what they thought when a glimpse of the calf was made possible.

These fine Georgian houses in Cooks Row were demolished in the early 1960s to make way for flats. The street possibly took its name from Tristam Cook, an MP and leading member of the corporation.

The main attraction at the seaside must surely be the donkey rides. This photograph was taken in about 1922 on the South Sands and shows 'Donkey' Elliot (with beard) and 'Ma' Elliot standing next to him. In the background can be seen the newly opened Futurist Picture House.

Before the visitors arrived the piers and Sandside looked peaceful and quiet. The ice house chimney can be seen towering above the property on Sandside which today consists mainly of amusement arcades.

Richardson's butchers, 66 Falsgrave Road is seen here in 1929. The staff posing outside are, left to right: George Tate, John Butler (whose family ran the Pigeon Pie at Sherburn), Fred Pottage and Arthur Umpleby, who will be remembered by many Falsgrave residents for his own butchers business which he opened at Seamer Road Corner.

Two forms of transport are seen on this photograph taken on the Foreshore in about 1930. The trams, never a financial success, disappeared in 1931 and the bus companies enjoyed a boom that lasts to this day.

Planks of wood are shoring up this very old property in Chapel Road. Not many people will know where this street was as it now forms part of Boyes car park.

Forge Valley has always been a rural retreat for Scarborians. The relaxing bubbling of the River Derwent and the beauty of the many trees and wild flowers make this area a paradise. Seen crossing the river after a flood had washed away the bridge in 1926 are from left to right: Charlie Pearson, George McKinley, George Moorhouse, James Percy, George Hogg, Gilbert Dobson, Percy Taylor, -?-.

The flapper influence is seen in this wedding photograph at St Mary's church in 1926. No long gown for the bride, although the older members of the family are still attired in an earlier style of dress.

Falsgrave School's uniform is shown on this young girl taken in the Bowling Green in 1924. The colour was navy blue with a yellow badge. This colour was still being used when the school closed down in the late 1960s. One part of the school was demolished in 1991 and houses were built on the site.

The British Legion Club had it headquarters at 21 Falsgrave Road when this photograph was taken in 1929. Members are displaying their billiard shield in the grounds of the house. Standing far left is Lieut.-Com. George Glenton, founder of the Legion. Seen also on the picture are Mr David Hunt, Mr Harold Coleman, Mr Joe Lever and John and Arthur Pottage.

The railway goods yard is shown here in the 1920s before mechanized transport took over from the horse. Over the years much traffic was handled there until the closure of the Whitby line in the mid-1960s seriously affected the movement of freight. In 1990 the whole area was demolished and its future is still uncertain.

The Albemarle scout group pose with their shield in the church hall in 1926. Back row, left to right: Jimmy Bean, James Percy, George Moorhouse, Jimmy Newstead, Maurice Webster. The three boys in the front row are unknown.

The ballroom of the Pavilion Hotel was always packed with enthusiastic dancers, keen sporting people of every sort and young people who made it their rendezvous.

The Spa waters had been taken as a cure since their discovery in the 1600s. They were said to 'communicate a sensible alacrity to the mind and a due tone to the elasticity of the stomach'. As the fashion declined a bandstand was erected over the pump room in 1875 and remained until 1931. Today there is no sign of the pump room although it still lies beneath the pavement.

Local talent under the leadership of the Revd Hugh Parry and Miss Joan Beattie performed in the historical pageant *The Mayflower* at the Opera House in February 1928. Members of the cast included Elsie Edwards, Elsie Nendick, Nell Stokes, J.W. Hebden, G.N. Hopper, J.G. Lyons and Lynwood Robinson.

The Prince of Wales Gardens on the South Cliff were very popular in the 1920s when this photograph was taken, perhaps more so than today. One feature of these gardens, long since gone, were the basket chairs upon which these two ladies are seated.

Taken from the Castle Hill in about 1935 this photograph shows the fine sweep of the bay looking towards the South Cliff. The yacht moored on the pier appears to be that of Captain Peel who visited Scarborough each season for the tunny fishing.

'Unrivalled in the history of watering places' was praise indeed when the Lord Mayor of London uttered these words in 1880. This view taken in the late 1920s outside the Green Lounge Cafe on the Spa only proves true the saying, 'The Spa was Scarborough and Scarborough was the Spa.'

Queen Street Central Hall's choir poses outside the building on 29 June 1931 after special services had been held to celebrate the opening of a new choir organ. This organ was to stand as a memorial to the twenty-three men of the church congregation who fell in the First World War.

A street party was held by the residents of Dumple Street to celebrate the demolition of the old street and the construction of the new Friargate. Lizzie Richardson organized the tea-party, and seen seated first right is the future mayor of the town, Johnny Jackson. By the mid-1930s the residents had settled into their new homes.

This view of Vernon Place taken in the 1920s is totally unrecognizable today. The buildings were demolished and extensions built on to the Mechanics' Institute which is seen on the left. On 19 June 1930 Sir Meredith Whittaker opened the greatly renovated building as the town's first public library.

Taken in the town hall in about 1932, these young ladies are being taught the skills of waitressing. The only face known is that of Rose Carvill seated first right.

Picturesque Falsgrave is seen at its best with this row of quaint cottages at the corner of Scalby Road. The first white cottage was the home of 'Donkey' Elliot whom we have met in an earlier photograph. The entrance on the far left leading between the houses led into Shield's Yard where half a dozen minute cottages stood. Today the whole area is a car park.

The Jolly Rogers Bathing Club is seen here on the South Sands on Christmas Day, 1934. Come rain or shine these healthy specimens could be seen on the beach. Among the robust members can be seen Sally Marlow, Bill Johnson, Eric Oldham and Avie Parr.

Pupils of St Mary's School, Queen Street, crown the Rose Queen at a ceremony in the playground in 1934. From left to right: Mary Wilkinson, Sheila Showers and Barbara Wilkinson. Far right is Barbara Grey with Barbara Stokes standing next to her. The Wilkinson girls' parents had the Equestrian pub on St Thomas Street. The school was demolished in 1970.

The crowning of the Rose Queen was a feature of the Scarborough season throughout the 1930s. Looking stunning in picture hat and taffeta dress is Miss Jean Graham acting as a rose queen attendant in 1934.

Hello there. Miss Dorothy Stokes with fashionable kiss curl sits in the Holbeck Gardens in 1930. Below her is the South Bay swimming pool that was opened in 1914.

Springfield at the corner of Longwestgate was typical of the many streets that made up the old town. The pub on the right was the Scarborough Castle but always known to the locals as 'The Shalla Watta'. The plaque on the first house in Springfield appears to give the letters ED and is dated 1765. As with most of this area it was demolished in the early 1960s.

Church Stairs Street leading up to the parish church has a long and varied history. It was in this street that John Wesley, the founder of Wesleyan Methodism, preached at a newly erected church in 1772. The church in time became tenements and was demolished, as was all the property in this street.

A Red Cross dinner at the Grand Hotel in about 1932 saw the guests in a mixed attire of uniforms, evening dress and day wear. Mr and Mrs Wherritt who ran a fancy goods shop in Eastborough are seen standing far left.

Cross Street was demolished around 1934 and one can see the old property in this photograph that made up the street. The Futurist Picture House is advertising Tom Walls in *Just Smith*; prices 1s 6d, 1s, 9d and 6d.

All aboard for the *Royal Lady*. This vessel was just one of the many pleasure boats that have plied their trade from Scarborough over the years. Her first trip from the resort was in 1934. She sailed for Malta in about 1938 and was sunk by enemy action during the war. The second *Royal Lady* arrived in 1938 and later served her country by taking part in the Dunkirk evacuations.

This superb aerial view of the South Sands captures the imposing Grand Hotel, Gala Land, the Cliff Bridge and many more features of 1936.

Picture hats, cocked at a jaunty angle, ankle-length frocks and clutch handbags were all the rage in 1937 when this photograph was taken down in the Glen. The Glen was originally known as Wilson's Wood and was transformed by Mr Harry W. Smith in about 1912 into an area of beauty with decorative pagodas, waterfalls and winding paths.

The famous Jowett car with its 'Dicky' seat was a favourite with families who wished for a compact and inexpensive vehicle. Seen at the wheel is Clara Cooper and her son Robert.

Exclusive South Cliff was popular with both local and visitor alike. This photograph taken in 1937 shows a young lady sitting on the balustrade which came from the Westfield Hotel, demolished to make way for the construction of Northway in 1930. To this day one can make out the name of the hotel on the end pillar.

Lest we forget. On a cold, wet Remembrance Day Sunday in 1936 the surviving members of the Scarborough Pals' Battery march in respect past the war memorial on Olivers Mount.

A double-decker Leyland Titan of 1935 makes its way towards Valley Bridge. The rounded top was designed especially to allow access under the arch at Beverley.

The Pavilion Vaults were always a popular meeting place for locals. In this photograph taken in 1936 Mr Arthur Midgley, who worked at the Pavilion Hotel, poses behind the bar at the request of Charles Laughton who had brought a film crew to the hotel for a series of film shots.

Unsettled times. The day that the author's parents were married at the parish church on 28 September 1938 Prime Minister Neville Chamberlain was in Germany for the Munich talks. His jubilant return to Great Britain with the infamous piece of paper declaring 'Peace in our time' followed.

Choirs gathered at Queen Street Central Hall on 22 May 1938 in celebration of the bi-centenary of the conversion of John Wesley. Here the choir display the Sir William Middlebrooke Shield. Dr R. Walker-Robson was the adjudicator for the musical events and Mrs Jessie Riley accompanied him.

A single-decker Leyland Tiger bus of 1937 is seen here parked outside the bus station in Somerset Terrace. Scarborough is now without a bus station – the Somerset Terrace depot closed in 1991.

Members of the church perform in *Wedding Banquet* on 18 March 1938 at Queen Street chapel, the proceeds of which were donated to the Northstead New Methodist Chapel Fund. The bride was Mrs L. Gill and the groom Mr J. Pollard. The bridesmaids were the Misses Rita Foord, Mary Wilkes, Edith Harrison, Jessie Newstead and Laura Jackson. Mr J. Todd was the best man and Messrs N. Newham, J. Rigby and G. Tomlinson were the groomsmen. The parents' parts were taken by Mrs Berry, Mr Tilbrooke, Mrs Mace and Mr Foord.

A summer's day in the Glen brings out the latest 1938 fashions. This dress worn by Miss Frances Pottage in red, grey and blue would have cost anything from 12s to £3, which was the average price of a dress in those days.

The Second World War

War was declared upon Germany on Sunday 3 September 1939 and at dinner time on the same day the sirens wailed out in town. No incident occurred but it was a foretaste of things to come.

Scarborough Amateur Operatic Society's production of *The Bohemian Girl* was cancelled due to the war situation. Seen here on the stage of the open-air theatre are some of the ladies of the cast, including Winnie Ireland, Emma Jones, Violet Archer and Joyce Dixon.

The South Sands on Bank Holiday Monday 1939 sees the seafront packed with visitors. The same view taken on the same day the following year shows a different picture as the war's grip slowly strangles the holiday trade.

The local defence volunteers, later to be renamed the Home Guard, were formed in May 1940. They trained on the cliffs above Scalby Mills and used the quarry at Olivers Mount for rifle practice. A typical guard consisted of three seventeen-year-olds and an older man. In the early days their weaponry usually took the form of two twelve bore shotguns and an 1890s rifle. In time they became an efficient fighting force. At 12.30 a.m. on 8 September 1940 they were called out when the message 'Invasion Imminent' was received. The Home Guard officially ended as a fighting force on 2 January 1946. Posing for the camera are members of the 10th North Riding (Scarborough) Battalion Home Guard. Back row, left to right: Second Lieut. H. Jackson, Capt. B. Jackson, Lieut. W. Molyneaux, Lieut. F. Unwin, Lieut. W. Dent and Lieut. J. Allen. Front row: G. Holmes, Maj. A. (Turby) Smith, Maj. J. Ellis, Capt. A. Thornton and Capt. A. Thompson.

The first batch of evacuees arrived on 1 September 1939. Over the following months the town would play host to over 12,000 refugees. Seen walking along Hoxton Road are a group of evacuees from Hull and leading the party is Jillian Barton and her mother.

The first air raid on Scarborough occurred on 26 June 1940 when a large number of incendiaries and bombs were dropped around the Scalby and Burniston areas. Burniston Farm seen on the photograph suffered a direct hit which completely lifted the building and dropped it again.

Anti-invasion obstacles were a common sight along the beaches during the war. I doubt if these few rolls of barbed wire and rubble seen on the North Promenade outside the Corner Cafe would have proved much of a deterrent to the enemy.

Scarborough's trawlers were often the targets for German aircraft as they flew along the coast. The *Silver Line* seen here at Ravenscar had a lively engagement with an enemy plane on 3 April 1940. A 'Heinkell' which had been harassing shipping was intercepted by a 'Spitfire' which resulted in both aircraft being shot down. The *Silver Line* also fired her guns damaging the plane further. They then rescued five enemy airmen whom they brought into port.

Age was no barrier when these veterans of the 30th Battalion Green Howards volunteered for duty at the outbreak of war. They were stationed at the wireless station on Sandybed Lane (where Row Brow flats now stand). They were billeted in the orchard bungalow which stood behind the station. In time they were posted to Linton-on-Ouse, Dishforth, Starbeck, Sheffield POW camp and Withernsea. The only member of the battalion known is Mr Bruce-Bowling who is standing second on the left in the greatcoat.

A former pupil of the Graham Sea Training School, Able Seaman John Francis aged 23 of St Thomas Walk died of wounds in hospital at Yarmouth on 24 July 1940. He was mentioned in dispatches, the citation stating that this was, 'for good service of which His Majesty's high appreciation is thus recorded'.

This bunch of local lads are home on leave and enjoying a drink in the Pavilion Vaults. Back row, left to right: 'Killer' Kennedy, Harry Smith, George Westwood, Edgar Kay, Jimmy Sheader, Fred Burton and Billy Westwood. The young man at the front is Jack Drydale and all of them came from the old part of town.

Static water tanks to deal with incendiary attack were a common sight in wartime Scarborough. This one in a passage off St Thomas Street was just one of the fifty placed at strategic points.

Shovelling snow in the cold winter of 1944 outside his home at the bottom of Mount Park Road is a future town councillor, Michael Pitts. Notice the white bands painted on the posts to assist people during the black-outs.

One of the fishing fraternity is Mr Tommy
(Pat) Rowley who served on the *Emulater* until
he was called for war service.

Moored at the lighthouse pier is the steam trawler *Emulater*. During the early days of the
war she had many lucky escapes when she was attacked by German planes. The crew of
the *Emulater* in 1940 were: Skipper, Alf Cox; Mate, Frank Eade; Deckhands, Tommy
Wison, Tom King and Tommy Rowley; 3rd hand, Bill Carsey; Engineers, George Skelton
and George Doy; Fireman, Jack Skelton; and Cook, G. Whittleton. The boat was broken
up in 1960.

A deadly weapon. Just after 9 p.m. on 10 October 1940 a lone raider swooped over the Castle Hill and dropped a land-mine on the densely populated old town. The crater in Potter Lane measured 60 ft across and 30 ft deep. Four people died as a result of this raid and over 500 houses were either damaged or destroyed. This view taken from the Castle Hill shows the damage to Potter Lane and Anderson Terrace.

Newly built houses in Potter Lane are shattered by the blast of the land-mine. Mr Charles Day in trilby hat looks around at the devastation. These houses had only been built two or three years before by Mr Day who undertook the job of rebuilding them.

Soldiers and civil defence workers inspect the ruined houses in Potter Lane after the raid. Over 300 men were engaged on clearance work, and on 8 November Royal Engineers demolished dangerous property in the area.

Potter Lane has been cleared of the rubble and the belongings of the families stored in St John's church. Some months later the church caught fire when a shower of incendiaries fell through the roof and many of the stored personal effects were lost.

Shorts Gardens suffered severe blast damage from the Potter Lane mine and was demolished at a later date. Standing outside her ruined house is Mrs Griffiths.

Castlegate was another street that suffered in the October raid. As with most of the property damaged by the blast Castlegate was demolished and new houses built.

Minutes after leaving her moorings in the harbour on the morning of 16 October 1940 the trawler *Pride* struck a mine in the harbour mouth. The skipper, William Johnson Colling, and his crew, William Colling, Frank Crawford and Jack Robinson, were all killed. In the background can be seen the destroyer *Walrus* that went aground on the Mascus Rocks in 1938 and was towed into the harbour.

Down in the harbour Mr 'Pat' Rowley is a well-known face. He knew all the members of *Pride*'s crew before the war.

Commercial Street was a quiet, everyday suburb off Falsgrave until the night of 18 March 1941. This night, that became known as the 'March Blitz', saw the town subjected to over four hours of intensive aerial bombardment as ninety-eight German planes flew back and forth across the borough. A large bomb struck this terrace of houses resulting in the deaths of seven people. The top photographs shows the houses in more peaceful days and the one below, the damage caused by the explosion.

For displaying courage when her home in Commercial Street was bombed in the March Blitz, twelve-year-old Margaret Willis received the Gilt Cross, the Girl Guides' highest award, from Lady Downe at a ceremony held at All Saints church hall on 18 May 1942. Margaret had been trapped along with her parents and little sister for over nine hours under the rubble. She had comforted her badly injured parents until they could be rescued. She is seen here with her mother and father proudly wearing the cross.

Fifty years on, Mrs Margaret Shaw still treasures the award.

Blazing inferno. Shortly after 8.45 p.m. on 18 March 1941, in the heaviest raid on the town, hundreds of incendiaries rained down on the printing works of E.T.W. Dennis & Sons in Melrose Street. Soon the blaze was out of control and firemen battled under falling bombs to check the spread. The building was completely destroyed and new premises were built on the site shortly afterwards.

Members of the AFS pose next to their fire appliance in the fire station yard. The fire chief, Mr Clark, is seated centre with Jim Russell to his left. Holding the station cat, who often went to many fires fast asleep on the engine, is Billy Pottage.

An aerial view such as this of the South Bay would be what the German pilots would look for as they made their way inland to bomb important targets.

The Queen's Hotel, North Marine Road dated back to the 1850s. On the night of the 'March Blitz' an HE bomb demolished the property opposite killing the family of six and a maid. The blast from this bomb caused extensive damage to the hotel. This, and the damage caused by the billeted troops, resulted in the decision to demolish the building after the war. Today The Cricketers public house stands on the site.

Queen Margaret's School on the South Cliff received a direct hit with a land-mine on the night of the blitz. A dance which had been arranged for that night had luckily been cancelled. The girls had been evacuated some time previously to Castle Howard.

Scarborough by night in pre-war days was a picturesque sight with the lights shimmering on the water. It was to be six long years before the illuminations could be turned on again.

The personnel of the ARP are lined up with their vehicles outside their headquarters in Grange Avenue. The only person known is Mary Drake (now Riby) standing fifth from the right.

Wartime fashions are seen in this photograph taken in about 1943. Notice the lady's brooch – the RAF wings – a present from her husband.

Although many men were in reserved occupations as was this gentleman, their determination to enlist got them accepted in the end. Here we see the RAF uniform of those years.

Leighton House flats at the corner of Brunswick Terrace and Vernon Road suffered blast damage from a sharp raid on 10 May 1941 when over 150 premises were damaged or destroyed. This building was demolished in 1946 and Brunswick Terrace in the late 1980s to make way for the Brunswick Pavilion.

A heavy bomb fell opposite this house at 14 The Crescent on 10 May 1941 blasting a deep crater in the public gardens and splattering the house with shrapnel, the scars of which can still be seen to this day.

Air-raid shelters such as this one at the Mere Bridge were a common sight in all the town's public gardens. It was only after the 'March Blitz' that street shelters were erected. In all over 1,500 were built and when they were demolished in 1946 the cost of dismantling them amounted to £8 each one.

Friarage School Army Cadets are seen here in 1942 proud to be doing their bit for King and Country. Some familiar faces are Raymond Jewison (drum major), Capt. West, Stan Mattison, Jim Firman, Austin Adamson, Bill Newiss, Jack Ellard, Bill Mennell (base drummer), Ray Pinkney, H. Jewison, Frank Winpenny and Charles Cooper.

Plaid frocks were all the fashion during the war years. When clothes rationing was introduced one was allowed sixty-six coupons to last the year. For example, a coat costing 79s 6d could only be purchased by surrendering sixteen clothing coupons. It was, therefore, essential to make one's clothing last.

Home on leave, this soldier of the Durham Light Infantry poses for an official photograph.

The Grand Restaurant below the Grand Hotel was built in 1871. Extensions were added in 1876 and it became a roller-skating rink. It remained as a rink until 1914 when the premises were converted into a picture house. During the Second World War the military requisitioned the building and it was used as a store. A serious fire broke out in the early months of 1942. It remained in a dilapidated state until 1949 when it was demolished. It is still an open space to this day and is the cause of much discussion.

Flying over Scarborough in an army Lysander Co-operation aeroplane on 4 June 1941, Pilot Officer Geoffrey Mould and his co-pilot headed in the direction of Lowdale Avenue where he lived. Circling his plane and losing height in doing so, he was unable to gain control. The plane crashed into the chimney of No. 26 Lowdale Avenue and plunged into an allotment garden killing both airmen.

A tip and run raid on a quiet Sunday evening of 14 September 1941 resulted in the destruction of four houses in Prospect Mount Road and the death of Mrs Nellie Thornton as she rode by on her bicycle. Woodlands Ravine railway bridge pictured here shows the scars from one of the bombs that blocked the rail link to Whitby for hours. Ten-year-old Dorothy Adamson (now Bullamore) who was passing at the time was blasted into the crater and suffered injuries to her legs and back.

Sunday evening chaos. At about
8.30 p.m. on 14 September 1941 a lone
raider swept in from the north. Banking
about Manor Road it released two
bombs, one of which fell on the
pavement outside Nos 1 and 3 Prospect
Mount Road. Four houses were
demolished and 40 ft flames shot into
the air from a shattered gas main. Mr G.
Duck was first on the scene followed by
Mr Brown who assisted in rescuing the
shocked, but unhurt residents.

Built originally as the Municipal School to a design by E.T. Hall, Cooper and Davis in 1899, the building in time became the Boys' High School. During the war years the school hall doubled as a training centre for the Army Cadet Force. In 1959 the Boys' High School moved to a new building and their old school became Westwood County Modern and remained so until its closure in 1973. Today the old building is The Theatre in the Round, home of Alan Ayckbourn's plays.

The Albert Hall, one of the town's first Liberal clubs on Aberdeen Walk, suddenly collapsed on the Monday afternoon of 14 July 1942. Clouds of dust and rubble invaded neighbouring property but as the building had been empty at the time no casualties occurred. Upon investigation it was found that the air raid of the 10 May 1941 had caused structural damage resulting in the collapse.

Pupils from the Friarage and Old Central Schools in their army cadet uniforms pose in the school playground in 1942. Capt. West is seen seated centre.

Beating the drum at the cricket ground in 1942 are boys of the Friarage and Old Central Schools. Leading the group is the drum major, Raymond Jewison.

Ye Olde Booke Stall was set up outside the main entrance to the town hall on 24 July 1942 in an effort to collect as many books as possible for salvage. The deputy mayor is seen here with Johnny Jackson, a future town mayor, standing to his left. At the end of the drive over 160 tons of books had been handed in.

Falsgrave's Special Constabulary are seen here posing for an official photograph at Christmas 1942. Included in the group are Inspectors Howe and Smith, Sergeants Bateman, Tennant, Woodhead, Kemshall and Smith and Specials Atkinson, Colledge, Cooper, Daniel, Davenport, Leadbeater, Moorhouse and Nelson.

St Martin's Players and members of the Green Howards performed *Bats in the Belfry* at the Arcadia Theatre in March 1943. The producer of this three-act play was Peggy Noble. Taking part in this particular sketch are first left, Robert Shebheare, fifth left, Gwynne Michael Nelson Griffiths, sixth left, Phyllis Frost (wife of the Adjutant 161 Regiment), Lieut. Maynard (standing in evening suit). Other members of the cast were G. Atterton, Phyllis Sealey, Jean Bowman, Patric Brady, Edward Gautry, Peter Salter, Kathleen Archer and Rheta Fewster.

The Sea Cadet Force was formed in January 1942 by Lieut. Com. Vincent Feather, headmaster of the Graham Sea Training School, to provide initial training for the Royal Navy. Seated here are: George Doy, Cyril Lamb, Fred Hall, Sid Bradley, Frank Bayes, 'Tubby' Furguson, 'Blondie' Wood, Reg Tymon, Charlie Plummer, Fred Coopland, John Morris, Dick Elliot and George Stewart.

The Scalby Fire Guards are seen here in the playground of what appears to be Scalby School in 1944.

The Olympia Ballroom and Restaurant was the most popular place of entertainment in town for both locals and the military. It had originally been built for a fisheries exhibition in 1895 and after being purchased by the corporation was converted into a ballroom in 1919. It was burnt nearly to the ground by a fire that broke out in the late 1970s under mysterious circumstances. Today, a whole new complex has arisen to take its place.

To escape the doodlebugs that were causing death and destruction in the southern counties Scarborough took in 1,200 evacuees. They began to arrive from Kings Cross on 20 July 1944. Seen on Sandside in these two photographs are Mr and Mrs Bowman and their children from London who were billeted with Mrs Morris in Auborough Street.

The wedding of Kathleen Morris to Fusileer Robert Thornham must rank as an achievement considering the time allowed for preparation. On 6 October 1944 a telegram arrived with the message 'Arrange everything for Monday 48 hour pass, Love Bob'. A special licence was obtained and neighbours rallied round with their coupons with which Kathleen purchased some rose pink material. Dolly Porter who lived nearby worked feverishly over the weekend to complete the dress. Mrs Wright, another neighbour, baked and iced a cake with ingredients from Hopwoods – a 'friendly' grocer. At 2 p.m. on 9 October 1944 they were married at St Peter's church, the bridesmaids being Netta Morris and Edie Leader.

The Balmoral Hotel, Westborough, was requisitioned by the military at the beginning of the war. This hotel was built in 1889 to a design by John Hall and Frank Tugwell and stood on the sight of The Bull Hotel. It was demolished in 1973 and a multi-storey car park built.

Christmas greetings came very official from the armed forces during the war. The seasonal message shown here was on a photocopied form which was issued to each member of the forces so preventing any leakage of information.

The Seaforth Highlanders' Pipe and Drum Band lead the march-past of various units of the armed forces past the dais where HRH The Princess Royal is taking the salute in Westborough on 17 June 1944 in connection with 'Salute the Soldier' Week. She then went on to inspect other members of the wartime services.

The foundation stone of the Jubilee Chapel, Aberdeen Walk was laid by Mr H. Hodge of Hull on 20 July 1860, the jubilee year of Primitive Methodism. The chapel was opened the following April. During the war years it was used as a rest centre for bombed out families. It was also 'home' for the boys of the Hull Trinity House Navigation School who were evacuated to Scarborough for the duration. The chapel was sold in 1964 and demolished two years later.

The Scarborough and District food office was situated on St Thomas Street. The staff between 1940 and 1945 were: Eric Horsfall-Turner, Charlie Whiteley, Fred Gregory, Clarence Cliff, Arthur Maynard, Walter Scott, Mr Hutchinson, Mrs C. Barnes, Mrs Crawford, Mrs Gill, Gladys Hodgson, Muriel Brown, Lily Gardener, Winnie Loy, Alma Colley, Joyce Dunning, Joyce Galley, Ellen Berry, Mavis Jewison, Kathleen Hutton, Joyce Clarke, Dola Bagshaw, Harriot Cass, Peggy Furness, Dorothy Smith, Mrs Midgley and Edith Clifford.

The Dean Road first aid post dealt with many air raid casualties during the war. Back row, left to right: M. Bremner, Stan Thompson, Miss Dawson, Mrs Boulder, Doris Wright, Miss Carr. Second row: Miss Jackson, Mrs Scarborough, Mrs G. Cooper, Miss Dixon, Mrs Smith, Mrs A. Smith, Mrs Wilson, Mr Stead. Third row: Mrs Atkinson, Miss Taylor, Mrs Cappleman, Miss Richardson, Mr E. Lee, Sister Holton, Mr Atkinson, Miss Chip, Mrs Shaw, Mrs Anderson, Mr Pell, Norah Brunney. Front row: Miss Whiting, Mrs Pell, Vera Midgley, Mr Cappleman, Ellen Berry, Mr Roberts, Alf Ruston, Gerry Cooper.

The burnt out shell of E.T.W. Dennis & Sons printing works is levelled by workmen.

Burniston Barracks was the home of the Seaforth Highlanders during their stay in Scarborough. This official photograph shows, back row, left to right: Bob Somers, Arthur Groom, Jack Perkins (all Yorks. and Lancs. lads), Bill Fisher (dance band leader). Front row: Eric C. Crook, Sgt. Sam Taylor, Orderly Room Sgt.-Maj. Joymer, E. Stephie, Bill Shelley, Bob Richardson.

The RAF B Flight, No. 11 Initial Training Wing were billeted at Bramcote School during 1944.

HRH The Princess Royal inspects members of the Red Cross on 17 June 1944 in the station forecourt. Seen standing at attention are: Mrs Chip, Miss Brown, Mrs Shaw, Mrs Pinder, Miss Taylor, Mrs Brown, Doris Wright, Mrs Smith, Mrs Richardson, Miss Cayley, Mrs Berry, Miss Jowsey and Mrs Atkinson.

After being captured in Libya, these three lads of the East Yorkshire Regiment – left to right: Ernest Sedman, Walt Adamson (both local boys) and Bill Kirk from Bradford – were route marched up through Italy and Germany to Stalag 8B at Lansdorf.

The sands were reopened to the public on 3 April 1942 between sunrise and sunset but no swimming was allowed. Sitting on the beach with the Futurist Picture House in the background is Mr George Heseltine, his wife Carrie and their two daughters, Pat and Dorothy.

The Opera House, St Thomas Street stands on the site of Adam's Circus which opened in 1877 and which became known as the Prince of Wales Circus the following year. It was then demolished and rebuilt and reopened as the Grand Opera House in 1908. Over the years such household names as Harry Lauder, Vesta Tilley, George Robey and Gracie Fields have appeared on stage. On 18 March 1941 the stage suffered considerable damage when a shower of incendiaries fell through the roof. True to tradition the show went on the following night on a makeshift stage built over the orchestra pit.

The auxiliary fire service personnel are seated at tables in their mess room above the fire station in North Marine Road some time in the early years of the war.

Members of the RAF No. 3 Flight, 3rd Squadron, Initial Training Wing pose in a public garden in 1944. This particular wing was billeted at the Grand Hotel.

Trafalgar Road's street party to celebrate VE Day, 8 May 1945, appears to have gone as planned to judge by the happy faces of the residents. The only two people known are Mrs Jessie Fox and her daughter Pat who went on to become the Mayoress of Chepstow.

Middle Walk's VE Day party shows a table laid out with what would have been the families' weekly food ration. Margaret Willis, who was bombed out of her home in Commercial Street and whose parents were allocated one of the Middle Walk houses, is seated centre in a white frock.

Mount Park Road's residents pose for their photograph taken after their VE Day street party. Among the faces can be seen Mr and Mrs Lickiss, Michael and Peter Pitts, Ann and Fay Rollett, Harry Stanworth and Mrs Maughan and her son Roger. There are also a number of evacuees on the photo who were billeted in the street.

St Mark's church schoolroom was the choice made by St Leonards Crescent's residents as the place to hold their VJ Day party on 14 August 1945. Seen outside the room are Betty Holmes, Mrs Mayes, Dorothy Adamson, Barbara Footitt, Eileen and Dougie Wedge, Mrs Burnett and Joyce Golder.

Hinderwell Road's street party is seen here in full swing. Three people are recognized: Sarah Hunter, standing first left, Mrs Hick in glasses next but one, and Bobby Cheetham in uniform on the far right.

The Green Howards march along Foreshore Road in 1945 to cheering from large crowds of spectators.

Local dignitaries and members of the armed forces gather in the town hall gardens on VE Day 1945 for a thanksgiving service.

In pouring rain on Sunday 13 May 1945 3,000 members of the armed forces marched to the railway station to take part in a thanksgiving service to celebrate the defeat of Germany.

A new generation arrived in 1945. Here we see the author with his mother in early 1946. Notice the fashionable 'Teddy Bear' coat with the padded shoulders.

The Sun Court on the Spa attracts many visitors each year who sit and relax to the music played by the resident orchestra. For twenty-five years Max Jaffa played on the Spa and he was greatly missed when he did not renew his contract. The Spa was extensively damaged on 27 February 1942 when a sea-mine exploded against the promenade wall.

The Post-war Years

The famous 'demob' suit is seen here on these three fisher lads from the old town after their return home in 1946. Left to right: Jack (Nobbler) Fletcher, Tom (Pat) Rowley and Jack (Bosun) Mann.

Given with pride. On Friday 26 October 1945 the Freedom of the Borough was conferred on the 5th Battalion, the Green Howards which allowed them the privilege of marching through the town with fixed bayonets, drums beating and colours flying. The men are seen here marching up Queen Street after the ceremony. The building on the right is the Convent and to its right, St Mary's School which was demolished in 1970. It is interesting to note that the railings on the houses along Granby Place on the left still remain and were, for some reason, not taken away for war salvage.

The staff of E.T.W. Dennis & Sons Ltd held their party to celebrate peace on 10 December 1945 at the factory in Melrose Street. Seen among the party-goers are Agnes Cammish, Ida Dundass, Betty Joyce, Enid Sedman, Ida Keith, Billy Monkman, Flo Palliser, Jenny Sheader and Frances Ward.

The Drum Head Service to celebrate peace took place on the South Sands on 8 June 1946. Members of the armed forces and civic heads were present and the destroyer, HMS *Diadem* was at anchor in the bay. Hymns were sung accompanied by Mr E. Robinson on the Hammond organ. A wreath was laid on the water as the 'Last Post' was sounded.

Paradise is a picturesque approach to Castlegate from the parish church, more so when these cottages lined the route. The property lies empty in this view and was demolished by the early 1960s.

The Spa Ballroom was built in 1924 and over the years many well-known bands, including Joe Loss, Kenny Ball and Scarborough's own Geoff Laycock, have played for the dancers. The refurbishment programme of the early 1980s greatly improved the ballroom's layout.

St Thomas Street was originally called Tanner Street until the early nineteenth century. Today there is little remaining of the old street. The property on the left was demolished and the YMCA built in recent years.

The destroyer HMS *Diadem* anchored in the bay as part of the 'Welcome Home' Week programme on 14 September 1946 in honour of the local servicemen and women who were arriving home after being demobbed.

Hope's Cottages above Longwestgate were demolished in the early 1960s as part of the redevelopment programme in the East Ward. Today an empty space remains.

The Uplands along Hackness Road was a stately residence standing in its own grounds and belonged to the racehorse owner, Miss Dorothy Robinson. When the property was sold it was converted into a school and remained as such until its demolition in the 1960s.

The Snowdrift Laundry staff of 1945 included a number of Ukrainian girls who had fled Europe at the end of the war. Back row, second from left: Jock Ferguson; sixth from left: Alf Dyer; eighth from left: Billy Pottage. Second row, third from left: Miss Davis; seventh from left: Edna Watson; twelfth from left: Lily Mulvana; sixteenth from left: Mary Winn. Third row: the Ukrainians. Fourth row, first from left: Charlie Moisley; second from left: Alfred Rumford; sixth from left: Hilda Davis; seventh from left: Arthur Somers. Front row, left to right: Miss Wright, -?-, -?-, Alice Rogers, -?-, Miss Moment (secretary), John Kennedy (owner and future mayor), Jackie Place.

The Cambridge Hotel standing in its prime position next to Balgarnie's church on Ramshill Road was opened to the public on 1 August 1866. It remained a popular hotel well into the present century. During the 1940s it suffered fire damage and a modernization programme was proposed. The hotel never did regain its popularity and in 1962 it was taken over by American technicians who moved in. By 1965 structural defects had been discovered and it was classed as unsafe. The only solution was to demolish the building and work commenced straight away. The site remained derelict until 1985 when the foundation stone was laid for a block of flats.

Nursing cadets of the British Red Cross spent a week in Scarborough in April 1950 and took part in various events including visits to the hospital and other establishments. These two photographs show local members at the Odeon cinema; one group in the foyer and the other in front of the stage where an unidentified dance band has been entertaining.

Van men from the Snowdrift Laundry pose with the firm's vans outside the premises on Scalby Road in 1946. The two centre vehicles had been requisitioned by the army for the duration.

Scalby Mills with its old world inn, bubbling stream and picturesque cliff walks was taken over by the Home Guard during the war and used as a training ground. To this day the rifle range can still be seen. Today the area is greatly commercialized and the building of the controversial sewerage plant has taken away the rural charm.

The Londesborough Theatre, Westborough was described as being the best specimen of architectural design in Scarborough when it was built in 1871. The theatre could seat 1,200 people and over the years such names as Oscar Wilde, Beerbohm Tree and Sir Charles Halle have associated themselves with the place. In July 1914 the Londesborough Theatre was converted into a picture house and remained so until it was demolished on 4 March 1960.

The Peoples' Palace and Aquarium was designed by Mr Birch who had been responsible for the construction of the Brighton Pavilion. Costing £100,000 to build and covering an area of 3 acres, the grand opening took place in 1875. This view taken about 1952 shows the Aquarium top looking towards the swimming pool. In 1969 the whole area was demolished and a car park constructed.

Foreshore Road is hardly recognizable on this photograph taken about 1953 compared with the busy thoroughfare of today. Just visible in St Nicholas Gardens is the spaceship in which, for a few pennies, one could be whisked off to faraway galaxies via a television screen.

The Turkish influence was very evident in the design of the interior of the Peoples' Palace and Aquarium. Over 5,000 persons could be accommodated in its murky depths. One could enjoy the many side-shows, view a working model of the Niagara Falls, or visit a monkey house and the shooting galleries. In 1880 Captain Webb swam for over 74 hours in the 75,000 gallon capacity tank. In 1886 the Aquarium was bought by Mr W. Morgan, a future mayor of Scarborough. By 1914 the company was in financial difficulties and in 1921 the corporation took over the running of it and renamed it Gala Land. It became a favourite with locals and visitors alike. An all-woman orchestra played in the theatre and there were bumper cars and various other rides. Gala Land holds many nostalgic memories for many people even if it is just the distinctive smell of the place.

Scalby Show drew in crowds of people, not only from Scarborough, but from the surrounding district. This photograph taken about 1950 shows Mrs Mary Riby with poodle and Kerry Blue. She is wearing the 'new look' that had swept the country in about 1947, thus bringing a more flattering line to women's fashion and replacing the rather masculine short skirts and padded shoulders of those austere war years when clothes rationing had dictated design.

The Constitutional Club, Huntriss Row was opened by the 3rd Marquess of Salisbury on 20 December 1888. Over the years it has been used for many functions including dances and jumble sales. Seen here at a Christmas party in about 1949 are Lilian Smith and Clara Cooper. The slightly inebriate-looking gent in the middle – or could he just be overpowered by the ladies' presence? – came from York.

Scarborough welcomed the arrival of the destroyer HMS *St James* on 4 July 1947. The commander, J. Lee-Barker, and his officers were guests of honour at a lunch given by the mayor, Alderman J. Jackson, at the Prince of Wales Hotel.

Lower Conduit Street is now renamed Princess Square but to the locals it will always be known as 'City Square'. During the 1960s the old houses were demolished and rebuilt in a style that blended in fairly well with the other property in the area. On the left is Pump Hill that leads down to Sandside and just visible at the corner of the house is the old Butter Cross.

All Saints church, Falsgrave was built in 1867 to a design by G.F. Boddy. The foundation stone was laid by Lord Hotham and the church consecrated by the Archbishop of York in 1868. When the evacuees arrived in 1939 they were taken here to be given refreshments before departing for their billets. The church was demolished in the late 1970s and flats were built.

Butlin's Holiday Camp, Filey was the venue for the Red Cross Conference on 10 June 1949. Work had started on the camp in 1939 but had been suspended for the duration. It was then taken over by the military and at one time or another Canadian and Jamaican airmen were billeted there.

The Cash Supply Stores were situated at the corner of St Helen's Square and Eastborough. They were a popular firm and delivered to all outlying districts in vans such as this one seen parked on Sandside. Seen in the background is the Welcome Inn Restaurant and the Bethel Mission which closed in 1990 and is now a business outlet.

The wedding of Edward Midgley to Betty Cownley is the last of the four shown in this book. One can see just how much the fashion scene has changed over the twenty-five-year period. The '20s flappers, the '30s elegance, the '40s restricted lines and here on this photograph the '50s smart but severe look all have their own distinct style, and each is only part of the ever-changing world.

Hinderwell School was officially opened on 28 October 1932 by the Mayor of Scarborough, Alderman J.W. Butler, who was also chairman of Scarborough's education committee. The school could accommodate 350 infants and 350 juniors. The first junior headmaster was Mr G. McWhan. Seen in an infant classroom in 1952 are from left to right: Stephen Moore, Robin Peasnod, Terry Arbor and Richard Percy. The teachers at Hinderwell School during the 1950s were Miss Berryman, Mr Milnes, Miss Lister, Mr Pearson, Miss Farmborough, Mr Wison (who nearly set the school on fire with his pipe which had been left in his pocket), Mrs Sanderson and Mrs Westmoreland. Miss Rhodes was the infants' headmistress and Mr Catton was head of the juniors.

The Queen's coronation of 1953 saw the town come to life with street parties and other festivities to celebrate the occasion. The residents of Oak Road, Highfield and Grange Avenue organized a party and puppet show which was held in Londesborough Road railway excursion station. The puppet show was given by Mr George Hoggarth. Some familiar faces can be seen in the happy gathering including John Johnson, Pat Leng, Richard Stephenson, Richard Percy, Carolyn Street, Jean Tennent, Sylvia Hoggarth, Stan Farline, Alan and David Booth, Eileen Exley, Alan Hathaway, Mr Frank Thompson, Mr K. Street, Mr A. Summerscales and Mrs Rycroft.

I WISH TO MARK, BY THIS PERSONAL MESSAGE, my appreciation of the service you have rendered to your Country in 1939.

In the early days of the War you opened your door to strangers who were in need of shelter, & offered to share your home with them.

I know that to this unselfish task you have sacrificed much of your own comfort, & that it could not have been achieved without the loyal co-operation of all in your household. By your sympathy you have earned the gratitude of those to whom you have shown hospitality, & by your readiness to serve you have helped the State in a work of great value.

Elizabeth R

Mrs.E.Morris.

A personal message from Elizabeth R.

The South Bay. With the elegant Spa, armada of sailing ships and cobbles and the 300 ft Castle Hill with its ruins of a Norman castle one can understand the magical attraction that Scarborough holds over the visitor. The tower in the foreground was demolished in the 1920s to make way for a new ballroom which had been designed by Frank A. Tugwell.

Acknowledgements

I am indebted to Yorkshire Regional Newspapers and to Mr Richard Welford Smith, LBIPP, LMPA for their help, and to the following for allowing me access to their photographic collections:

Mrs Bourne • Mr W. Bruce-Bowling • Mrs Dorothy Bullamore • Mrs R. Carvill
Mrs Clara Cooper • Mr Eric Copeland Crook • Mr A.L. Day
Miss J. Davidson • Mrs Georgie England • Mrs J. Fairbairn • Mrs Pat Flemming
Mrs M. Green • Mr G. Nelson Griffiths • Mrs A. Hotchkins • Mrs Hurd
Mrs J. Johnson • Miss Emma Jones • Mr Arthur Midgley • Mrs Minnie Midgley
Mr Edward Midgley • Mrs Anne Mitchell • Mrs Netta Oliver • Mr James Percy
Mrs Frances Percy • Councillor Michael Pitts • Mr Frederick Pottage
Mr William Pottage • Mr Ivor Rees • Mrs Mary Riby • Mr Tommy Rowley
Mr R. Sample • Mrs Enid Sedman • Mrs Margaret Shaw • Mrs Meg Somers
Mr David Stokes • Mr B. Tashara • Mrs Kathleen Thornham
Mr Steve Turton • Mr Charles White
and to Mr Bryan Berryman, reference librarian, for his help.